ROMANS, ANGLO-SAXONS AND VIKINGS IN BRITAIN

HAYDN MIDDLETON

Heinemann

www.heinemann.co.uk/library

Visit our website to find out more information about **Heinemann Library** books.

To order:

☎ Phone 44 (0) 1865 888066

📄 Send a fax to 44 (0) 1865 314091

💻 Visit the Heinemann Bookshop at www.heinemann.co.uk/library to browse our catalogue and order online.

First published in Great Britain by Heinemann Library, Halley Court, Jordan Hill, Oxford OX2 8EJ, part of Harcourt Education. Heinemann is a registered trademark of Harcourt Education Ltd.

Editorial: Jilly Attwood, Kathy Peltan and Vicki Yates
Design: David Poole and Tokay Interactive Ltd
Picture Research: Hannah Taylor
Production: Camilla Smith

Originated by Chroma Graphics (Overseas) Pte. Ltd
Printed in China by WKT Company Limited

ISBN 0 431 07903 X (hardback)
10 09 08 07 06
10 9 8 7 6 5 4 3 2 1

ISBN 0 431 07909 9 (paperback)
10 09 08 07 06
10 9 8 7 6 5 4 3 2 1

British Library Cataloguing in Publication Data
Middleton, Haydn
Romans, Anglo-Saxons & Vikings in Britain
941'.01
A full catalogue record for this book is available from the British Library.

Acknowledgements
The publishers would like to thank the following for permission to reproduce photographs:
Alamy Images pp. **6**, **27** (Geogphotos); Ancient Art & Architecture Collection pp. **14**, **16**, **25**, **37** (Ronald Sheridan), **19**, **41t** (L. Ellison), **41b** (R. Thorne); Bridgeman Art Library p. **23** (British Museum); Corbis pp. **5** (Ted Spiegel), **8** (Angelo Hornak), **21t** (Philippa Lewis; Edifice); English Heritage Photo Library p. **36**; Harcourt Education Ltd pp. **9** (Kate Shemilt), **13** (Peter Evans), **17t**, **17b** (Terry Griffiths & Magnet Harlequin), **28** (Tudor Photography); Rex Features p. **4**; Roman Baths Museum, Bath & North East Somerset Council p. **21b**; The Art Archive pp. **11** (Bibliotheque Municipale Poitiers/Dagli Orti), **29**, **31** (British Library), **35** (Bodleian Library Oxford) **43** (Ashmolean Museum/Eileen Tweedy); Trustees of the British Museum pp. **15**, **20**, **22**, **24**, **30**; Werner Forman Archive pp. **10** (Musees de Rennes), **34** (Statens Historiska Museum, Stockholm), p. **33**; York Archaeological Trust pp. **39t**, **39b**.

Cover photograph of the Minerva mask, reproduced with permission of the Roman Baths Museum, Bath & North East Somerset Council.

The publishers would like to thank Robyn Hardyman, Bob Rees and Caroline Landon for their assistance in the preparation of this book.

Every effort has been made to contact copyright holders of any material reproduced in this book. Any omissions will be rectified in subsequent printings if notice is given to the publishers.

Any words appearing in the text in bold, **like this**, are explained in the glossary.

Contents

Exploring further

Throughout the book you will find links to the Heinemann Explore CD-ROM and website at www.heinemannexplore.co.uk. Follow the links to discover more about a topic.

What do the symbols mean?

The following symbols are used throughout the book:

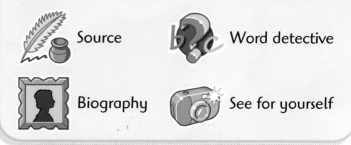

Source

Word detective

Biography

See for yourself

Why do people move away from where they were born?

Have you always lived in Britain? Have you come to Britain from another country? If you leave your country to live somewhere else you are **emigrating**. A new person in a country is called an **immigrant**.

Why do people emigrate?

Many people move to Britain to get a job. They may come for just a short time, or they may settle in Britain with their families and never leave. These people have chosen to emigrate.

In many of the biggest cities in Britain there are large communities of Chinese immigrants. They may create their own area in the city. This is London's Chinatown, which is full of Chinese shops and restaurants.

People flee to safety

Sometimes people have to emigrate. Think of the **refugees** who come to Britain from countries such as Afghanistan or Iraq. They come here because they are suffering in their home country. If there is a war where you live, or if life in your country has become very dangerous, you may feel you need to escape to somewhere safe. By becoming a **citizen** of a new country, you can try to make a fresh start.

Invaders and conquerors

Over the centuries, another sort of people have come to Britain from other countries. These people were armies of invaders. The invaders **conquered** all or parts of Britain, then lived here themselves. In this book you can find out about three groups of invaders: the Romans, the Anglo-Saxons, and the Vikings.

The carving on this tombstone shows Viking invaders with axes. It comes from Lindisfarne, one of the first places in Britain to be attacked by the Vikings.

Exploring further

The Heinemann Explore website and CD-Rom are divided into separate sections; one each for the Romans, the Anglo-Saxons, and the Vikings. As well as text on all the key topics, you can explore pictures, biographies, written sources and activities. Go to the Contents screen of the section you are interested in. Click on the blue words in the list and off you go!

Who invaded and settled in Britain a long time ago?

In the year AD 43, the Romans invaded Britain. They wanted to make it part of the Roman **Empire**. Britain was rich in corn, cattle, silver, and iron, so it was well worth **conquering**. The **Celtic tribes** of Britain did not want the Romans to settle. Some of them fought the Roman army.

The conquest begins

First the Romans conquered the south-east corner of Britain. Then they marched further north and west. As the Romans advanced, they built roads and forts. Soldiers in the forts kept the conquered lands under control. The roads helped them to travel quickly to troublespots. Soon most of southern Britain came under Roman control.

The Romans settle

The Romans mainly settled in the south of Britain. They called this land Britannia. They ruled over it for nearly 400 years. They often lived alongside the Celtic **Britons**.

The Romans built forts like Burgh Castle, on the east coast, to protect Britain from Anglo-Saxon raiders.

By AD 117, the Roman Empire covered most of Europe and parts of North Africa and the Middle East.

Roman Empire
— Hadrian's Wall

Invaders from the east

As other parts of the Roman Empire needed protecting, fewer soldiers were kept in Britain. Sea-**raiders** from Europe took advantage of this and began to attack. Some brought their families and settled in Britain. Some of the invaders were Angles, some were Saxons, some were Jutes. We call them all Anglo-Saxons.

A new threat

In AD 793, raiders attacked the **monastery** at Lindisfarne, a small island off the north-east coast of England. They were Vikings from **Scandinavia**. Travelling by land and sea, these Vikings terrorized parts of the world for about 300 years. In some places – including England – they settled and mixed with the local people.

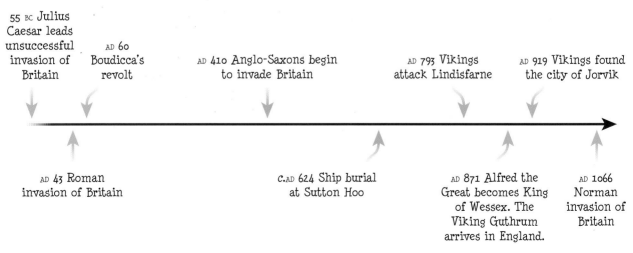

55 BC Julius Caesar leads unsuccessful invasion of Britain

AD 60 Boudicca's revolt

AD 410 Anglo-Saxons begin to invade Britain

AD 793 Vikings attack Lindisfarne

AD 919 Vikings found the city of Jorvik

AD 43 Roman invasion of Britain

c.AD 624 Ship burial at Sutton Hoo

AD 871 Alfred the Great becomes King of Wessex. The Viking Guthrum arrives in England.

AD 1066 Norman invasion of Britain

Who were the Celts and who were the Romans?

The **Celts** and the Romans were not very alike. Their ways of life were very different. They had different beliefs, languages, and clothes.

How do we know about the Romans and Celts?

The Romans liked to read and write. They wrote many books about the Roman way of life. The Celtic **Britons** wrote very little down.
We only know about their lives from Roman writings, and from things that **archaeologists** have found.

Where did they live?

Many Celts lived in settlements on the tops of hills. These were well defended against attack, with ditches, and with earth and stone walls. There were wooden houses with thatched roofs. Some Celts also lived in small villages or on individual farms.

The Romans mostly lived in towns with paved streets, public baths, and theatres.

Hundreds of people lived and worked in this **hill fort** of Maiden Castle, in Dorset. In workshops, craftsmen made iron and bronze tools, weapons, and jewellery.

The Roman general Julius Caesar wrote this after his visits to Britain in 55 BC and 54 BC. Archaeologists have found that, in fact, some inland **tribes** did grow crops.

*By far the most civilized natives are those living in Kent ... Most of the inland tribes do not grow corn, but live on milk and meat, and wear skins. All the Britons dye their bodies with **woad**. This makes them go blue, so that they look more terrifying in battle.*

How did they live?

The Celts lived mostly by farming. They grew crops and kept animals. Some were skilled metalworkers. They lived in tribes. These had their own laws and were led by a chief. They sometimes fought each other. They were not **primitive**, but were very different from the Romans. Celtic Britain had few roads. There was some trade in corn, gold, animals, and iron.

The Romans controlled a large **empire** across Europe. Most Romans lived in towns. These were linked by good roads. They had also developed useful technology.

Julius Caesar

Julius Caesar was a great Roman military leader, who **conquered** lands for the Roman Empire. He lived from 100 BC to 44 BC. In 55 BC and 54 BC he led his army in two unsuccessful invasions of Britain. He wrote about the people and places he found there. Caesar was murdered by a group of Romans who feared that he wanted to make himself king of Rome.

The Romans decorated the floors of their houses with beautiful **mosaics**. This one, from a palace at Fishbourne in Sussex, can still be seen today. It shows the Roman god Cupid sitting on a dolphin.

What did they believe?

The **Celts worshipped** many gods. Today, **archaeologists** still find things that the Celtic people left for their gods, such as carved animals, cups, and weapons. The Celts also thought that when someone died, their soul went into another body. This meant they were not afraid of dying.

Each Celtic tribe worshipped its own gods. This carving is of Brigantia, a goddess worshipped by the Brigantes tribe who lived in northern England.

The Romans also worshipped many gods. Even the emperor was treated as a god. The main Roman gods were Jupiter, Venus, Neptune, and Mars. Jupiter was the head of the gods. Venus was the goddess of love, Neptune the god of the sea, and Mars the god of war. To please the gods, the Romans killed cattle and sheep and poured wine on altars as **sacrifices**.

What was their language?

The Celts spoke their own language, but there is little evidence to show that they wrote things down. Famous events in their history would be told again and again in stories that were passed from one skilled storyteller to another.

The Romans spoke and wrote in **Latin**. They kept written records of their history and of the lands they made part of their **empire**. For example, a Roman geographer and historian called Strabo wrote about what he saw of Britain.

This example of Latin writing is from an 11th century manuscript.

Exploring further

Use the Heinemann Explore CD-ROM or website to find out more about the differences between the Celts and the Romans, in the Activity 'The Celts'. You have to write a guide for Roman soldiers to use, describing the appearance and way of life of the Celts.

11

Who was Boudicca?

Boudicca was a **Celtic** queen. She was married to Prasutagus, King of the Iceni **tribe,** and lived in the area that is now called East Anglia. Boudicca led a huge **revolt** against the new Roman rulers. This made her one of the most famous women in British history.

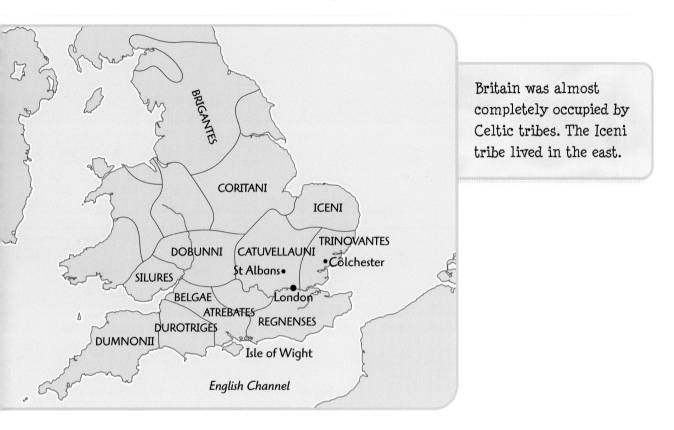

Britain was almost completely occupied by Celtic tribes. The Iceni tribe lived in the east.

Boudicca was a powerful and determined warrior and leader. Even so, at a great battle in the Midlands the Celtic **Britons** were defeated. Boudicca may then have poisoned herself.

Dio Cassius was a Roman historian who wrote about Boudicca 100 years after she was alive. This is how he described her:

'She had great intelligence ... She was very tall and grim; her gaze was sharp and her voice was harsh; she grew her long auburn hair to the hips and wore a large golden **torque** and a big patterned cloak.'

This bronze statue of Boudicca driving her chariot was put up in London in the early 1900s.

What Tacitus wrote

Tacitus was a Roman historian who lived soon after Boudicca's time. He wrote about what she did before the battle: 'Boudicca drove round all the tribes in a chariot with her daughters in front of her. "I am not fighting for my kingdom and wealth. I am fighting as an ordinary person for my lost freedom ... Consider how many of you are fighting – and why. Then you will win this battle, or perish. That is what I, a woman, plan to do!"'

Caratacus

Caratacus was leader of the Catuvellauni tribe in central England when the Romans arrived. He and his forces fought the Romans, but they were defeated. Caratacus fled north to join the Brigantes, but their queen, Cartimandua, was a friend of the Romans and she handed Caratacus over to them. Caratacus was sent in chains to Rome. He was later forgiven, and he lived the rest of his life in Rome with his family.

Exploring further

Use the Heinemann Explore CD-ROM or visit the website to find out more about how different Celtic tribal leaders reacted to the Roman invasion.

Try looking in 'Digging Deeper' for information about Cogidubnus, leader of the Atrebates of southern Britain, and Caswallawn of the Catuvellauni.

What happened in AD 60?

Some **Celtic tribes** gave in to the Romans and lived under their rule. Other tribes tried to fight the Romans. By AD 60, the Romans had almost won their long fight with the tribes of the west. This is when Boudicca and the tribes in the east decided to **revolt**.

Why did Boudicca revolt?

In AD 60, Boudicca's husband died. The Romans raided his land and homes. This made Boudicca very angry and she decided to fight back. Many tribes joined her. They did not like Roman rule either.

Boudicca and her army attacked the Roman towns of Colchester, London, and St Albans. Around 70,000 Romans and **romanized Britons** were killed.

Colchester was ruthlessly attacked by the rebels. This head of the statue of the Roman emperor Claudius from the temple was found in a nearby river in 1907.

What happened next?

The Roman army rushed back from the west. They met up with Boudicca's army in the middle of southern Britain, and went into battle.

The Roman writer, Tacitus, made the great battle of AD 60 sound easy for the Romans. He said that the Romans knew how to fight big battles and so killed many Celtic Britons. Dio Cassius wrote that the battle was hard for both sides: 'There was a mighty battle and equal spirit and daring were shown on both sides.'

However, in the end the British rebels did lose. Tacitus wrote that 'almost 80,000 Britons fell. Our own soldiers were 400 dead. Boudicca poisoned herself.'

We can learn about the Roman army from weapons that **archaeologists** find.

Exploring further

Use the Heinemann Explore CD-ROM or website to find out more about the terrible **massacre** that happened when the rebel forces reached London.

Look in 'Digging Deeper', The Roman conquest of Britain.

What were the short-term and long-term results of Boudicca's revolt?

In the short term, the Romans treated the **Celtic tribes** harshly. In the long term, however, they settled peacefully.

What happened after the revolt?

After the **revolt** of AD 60, thousands more Roman troops were sent to Britain. They took horrible **revenge** on the Celts. All through that winter the Roman ruler, Paulinus, and his soldiers kept attacking the tribes. The Celts had not been able to grow food while they were fighting the Romans, so many were starving.

Eventually the Romans realized that this would never make Britain **prosperous**. A new ruler, Turpilianus, was sent to Britain. He stopped the attacks. Slowly the **province** was rebuilt.

These gold Roman coins were found buried in Kent. Experts think they were the pay of a Roman soldier. He buried his money to keep it safe, but was then killed. Some of the coins show the head of the emperor. Coins are one kind of **artefact** that has survived well from Roman times.

A Roman Britain

The new Roman ruler sent people back to work, ploughing fields and rebuilding homes. The Romans tried to win the support of the Celtic **nobles**. They restored their wealth, so that they could enjoy the benefits of Roman rule. New Roman-style **villas** and towns were built to replace the ones destroyed in the revolt. The Romans never fully controlled northern Britain, but under Roman rule, southern Britain enjoyed 400 years of peace and prosperity.

See for yourself

Hadrian's Wall

To guard against future rebellion, the Roman army built more roads and larger fortresses. They also built Hadrian's Wall in northern England, to stop raiders attacking from Scotland. You can visit parts of Hadrian's Wall today.

The wall is 117 kilometres (72 miles) long, and stretches from one side of the country to the other. It was about 6.4 metres (20 feet) high. It was begun in AD 122 by order of the Emperor Hadrian. About 14,000 soldiers manned the wall. They lived in sixteen forts, like this one at Vindolanda, positioned along it.

How did the Romans change Britain when they settled here?

The Romans thought that their way of life was best. They wanted to teach others how to live like them. In Britain, the Romans brought many changes, but historians are not certain how much they changed daily life for most **Britons**.

Government

The most important person in Roman Britain was the **governor**. He probably lived mostly in or near London, the biggest city. He was helped by his staff of Romans, but also by **romanized** Britons. These were people who copied the Roman way of life and made sure it continued.

The Romans built a network of good, straight roads so that troops and goods could be moved quickly. This also made it easier for the **Celtic tribes** to make contact with each other.

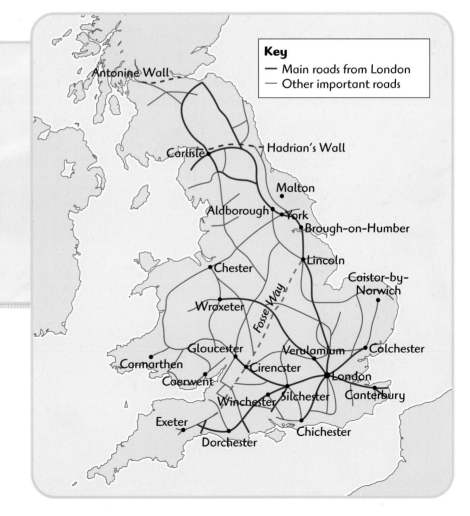

Key
— Main roads from London
— Other important roads

Antonine Wall
Carlisle
Hadrian's Wall
Malton
Aldborough York
Brough-on-Humber
Chester
Lincoln
Caistor-by-Norwich
Wroxeter
Fosse Way
Gloucester
Verulamium Colchester
Carmarthen
Cirencster
Coerwent
London
Winchester Silchester Canterbury
Exeter
Chichester
Dorchester

Towns and cities

Many Britons lived and worked in the countryside. They kept farming in their old ways, had little to do with the Romans, and never learned to speak **Latin**. The Romans built many new towns, such as Lincoln, Cirencester, Gloucester, and York. For the Britons living in towns, life changed much more.

Towns had streets in a grid pattern, and at the centre was the forum. This was a market place and meeting place. People also met to socialize at the public baths.

Sometimes Britons married Romans.
This gravestone of a British woman was found near Hadrian's Wall.
Her husband was an ex-soldier from Arabia. Her name was Regina,
which is the Latin for 'queen'.

In 1999, British historian Professor Muir Hunter wrote this about the effect that the Romans had on Britain:

*Britannia was one of the richest and most successful of the **provinces** ... The Romans' amazing road network is the basis of our motorways and main roads, and they made most rivers **navigable**. Their skilful farming produced great prosperity, and agricultural estates covered the country. Most of our cities were founded by the Romans ... Every town had public baths, every city an **amphitheatre**.*

Houses

Romans built their houses to last. They built town houses made of stone. Rich farmowners lived in country **villas**. The walls were decorated with paintings, and the floors with **mosaics**. Some houses also had glass windows and underfloor heating. The remains of over 600 Roman villas have been found in Britain.

Religion

The Romans did not want to upset the gods of the **Celtic Britons**. In some British temples, for example at Bath, both Roman and Celtic gods were worshipped. From about the 2nd or 3rd century AD, the Christian religion began to reach Britain. Early Christians in Britain were punished by the Romans because they would not worship Roman gods.

Exploring further

Use the Heinemann Explore CD-ROM or website to find out more about:

- the Roman palace at Fishbourne

- how the estate of a villa was run

- how the old religions clashed wit Christianity in Roman Britain.

Look in 'Digging Deeper'.

The Romans brought fine objects to Britain from other areas of the empire such as this glassware made in Italy.

See for yourself

Bath

The Roman name for Bath was Aquae Sulis, after Sulis, a Celtic goddess of the area. She was like the Roman goddess of healing, Minerva. The Romans built a temple to Sulis-Minerva over the local hot springs, which people thought could cure diseases. They also built a large series of baths there, which you can still visit today. People came from all over Europe to visit the temple and baths at Bath.

How was the grave at Sutton Hoo discovered and what was in it?

In the 5th and 6th centuries, many Anglo-Saxons settled in Britain. They came from northern Europe, and gradually took over the country. They did not write much about their lives during that time. We can only look at what **archaeologists** have found to tell us what their life was like.

An amazing discovery

In 1939, archaeologists began to dig into an ancient mound of earth at Sutton Hoo, in Suffolk. Mounds can sometimes have old graves in them. In **pagan** times, people used to bury objects with dead bodies.

The mound at Sutton Hoo was special, as the archaeologists dug they realised it was a ship burial. Many treasures were found. This showed that it was the grave of a wealthy person. Other ship burials had been found before, but none contained as many valuables as the one at Sutton Hoo.

Inside the mound, the shape of a ship could be seen. The ship's wood had rotted away, but its shape was still clear and the nails were still in place. The ship was nearly 30 metres (98 feet) long. In pagan times, important men were sometimes buried in ships to help them on their journey to the next life.

What was in the ship at Sutton Hoo?

In the middle of the ship were a variety of objects: a helmet, a sword with gold on it, an axe, a shield, spears, drinking horns with silver on them, bronze and silver bowls, silver spoons, a stringed instrument like a harp, beautiful jewellery, and a big purse containing 37 coins. There were also everyday things such as combs, board games, and buckets.

The coins were made between AD 620 and 640, which was in early Anglo-Saxon times. This is a clue to when all the goods were buried. Today you can see the objects from the Sutton Hoo burial at the British Museum in London.

These drinking horns were found among the treasure at the Sutton Hoo burial ship. Each horn held twelve pints, or nearly seven litres, of wine. Anglo-Saxon people probably drank a lot to quench their thirst, as they ate a lot of salty food.

Whose grave was it?

We do not know who was buried at Sutton Hoo. **Archaeologists** have used the things from the grave as clues to find out who it might have been.

Clues from the ship's cargo

The ship and its treasure cost a lot of money. Only a rich and powerful person would have had a grave like this. The person must have known people who lived outside Britain. Some of the things, such as coins, came from other countries. Only a rich person would have had these things.

This iron helmet from Sutton Hoo is decorated with scenes of fighting. It also has overlays of bronze, silver, and gold.

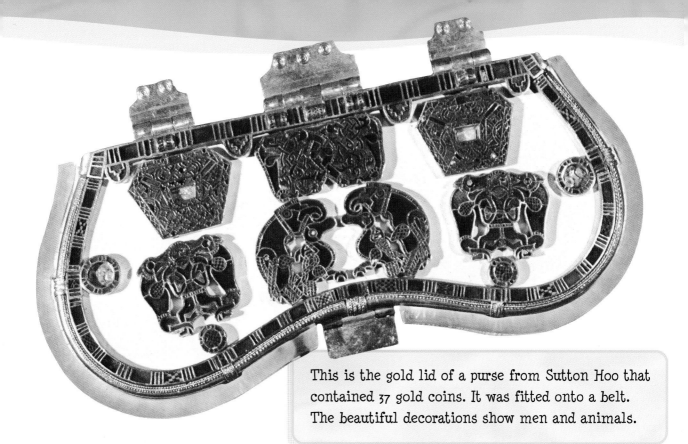

This is the gold lid of a purse from Sutton Hoo that contained 37 gold coins. It was fitted onto a belt. The beautiful decorations show men and animals.

Looking for a king?

In the 7th century, Sutton Hoo was in the kingdom of East Anglia. The richest and most powerful person in East Anglia was the king. Some people think the grave was for King Aethelhere, who lived around 655. He might have been killed in battle, and then his body was not found. Perhaps his people made the grave for him even though they could not bury his body.

Others think the boat was buried earlier and that the grave was for King Redwald of East Anglia who died in about 625. He was the most powerful king in Britain at that time. He would have had a very grand burial.

Exploring further

Use the Heinemann Explore CD-ROM or website to find out more about:

- the **reconstruction** of the helmet from Sutton Hoo, in a video clip

- the other powerful Anglo-Saxon kings at the time of the Sutton Hoo burial.

Look in 'Media Bank' and in 'Digging Deeper, Kings, chiefs and warriors'.

What was life like at the time the person in the grave was alive?

Anglo-Saxon England was divided into kingdoms. Each king's **warriors** were loyal to him in battle. In return he gave them land and riches. Some **Celtic Britons** lived alongside the newcomers. Others fled to the far west and north.

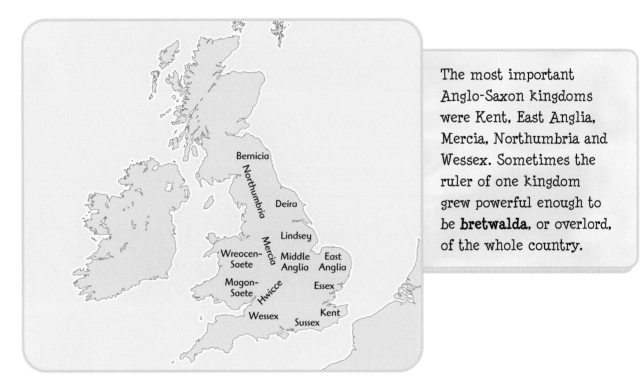

The most important Anglo-Saxon kingdoms were Kent, East Anglia, Mercia, Northumbria and Wessex. Sometimes the ruler of one kingdom grew powerful enough to be **bretwalda**, or overlord, of the whole country.

Monks, priests, and workers

Apart from the warriors, there were the monks and priests, who prayed, and the workers. Most workers were farmers, living in villages. They grew their own food. They ate mostly vegetables like cabbages, peas and beans, and fruit. Other workers were craftsmen or builders. Women worked in the home, looked after the family, and helped the men.

Exploring further

Use the Heinemann Explore CD-ROM or website to find out more about:

- how Anglo-Saxon houses were built and thatched
- how Anglo-Saxon villages were organized.

Look in 'Digging Deeper, Inside houses and homes'.

Homes and clothes

Most homes were made of wood, with a straw roof. Inside, a cooking pot would hang over a fire. There was little furniture.

Women wore a long gown fastened at the shoulder with a brooch. They also wore jewellery. Men wore short tunics over leggings, with leather laced boots.

See for yourself

West Stow, Suffolk

Many Anglo-Saxons lived in houses made of wood, with thatched roofs. Some houses had earth floors, while others had dug-out floors covered with wooden boards. The houses did not have windows or chimneys. A large cooking pot hung over a fire in the middle of the floor. Families often ate and slept on the floor.

Anglo-Saxon homes rotted away a long time ago, but in West Stow **archaeologists** have found traces of some Anglo-Saxon buildings. From the clues they have found, they have been able to reconstruct eight buildings using the tools and techniques that the early Anglo-Saxons might have used.

Beliefs

When the Anglo-Saxons first came to Britain they were **pagans**. In 597, Pope Gregory the Great in Rome sent **missionaries** to convert Britain to Christianity. They were led by Augustine. Other Christian missionaries came from Scotland. They were very successful, but some people still worshipped both pagan and Christian gods.

Word detective

The Anglo-Saxons named days of the week after their pagan gods. Tuesday is Tiw's day, Wednesday is Woden's day, Thursday is Thonor's day and Friday is Frigg's day.

The first Christian churches were built of wood. Later, they were built of stone. This early Christian church is in Hyde, near Winchester. The remains of Alfred the Great, the Anglo-Saxon King of Wessex from 871-899 are buried here.

Bede

Bede was a monk and a scholar. He wrote *The History of the English Church and People*, a book that tells us a lot about the early Anglo-Saxons in Britain. Bede was born in about 672. He was in touch with important people like kings, bishops and abbots, but he spent almost all his life inside **monasteries**. He died in 735. This picture of Bede is from a 12th century manuscript.

Trade and towns

Trade declined in Britain after the Romans left. The new Anglo-Saxon rulers encouraged trade once more. They ordered luxury goods, especially gold and silver jewellery, for themselves or as gifts for other leaders. Ports in south-east England, such as Dover, grew quickly, and coins were made there. Woollen cloaks, lead, cattle, and cheese were **exported**. **Imports** included Chinese silks, German swords, and wine.

As trade grew, so did the towns. Markets were held there to buy and sell goods. Trading towns were called 'wics'. Some town names still show this, such as Ipswich and Norwich.

This is what Bede wrote about London in about 731.

The capital of the East Saxons is the city of London. It stands on the banks of the River Thames and is a trading centre for many nations. They come to it by land and sea.

What have we found out about who was buried in the Sutton Hoo grave?

The beautiful objects found at Sutton Hoo tell us that the person buried there was rich and powerful, and a **warrior**.

These silver bowls from the grave show how important the person buried there was, as they were **imported** from Europe. They also suggest he may have been Christian, because they are decorated with crosses.

Redwald

Redwald was king of the East Angles in the early 7th century. Many historians think the Sutton Hoo burial was his. The monk and writer Bede tells us that Redwald was a **bretwalda**, a king who ruled over the whole country. He was baptized a Christian, but also continued to **worship** the old gods.

Beowulf

Lots of people must have helped to make the Sutton Hoo grave. We can try to picture it by reading an old Anglo-Saxon poem called *Beowulf*. It tells the tale of a warrior called Beowulf and his heroic deeds. It was written down some time between 650 and 1000.

In this part of the poem, Beowulf has just died. This is what his people, the Geats, did with his body. Perhaps this is what happened at Sutton Hoo:

*The Geat people built a **pyre** for Beowulf,*
stacked and decked it until it stood four-square,
hung with helmets, heavy war shields,
and shining armour, just as he had ordered ...
Then the Geat people began to construct
a mound on a headland, high and imposing,
a marker that sailors could see from afar,
and in ten days they had done the work ...
*And they buried **torques** in the barrow,*
and jewels ...

Exploring further

Use the Heinemann Explore CD-ROM or website to find out more about:

- how Anglo-Saxon place names have survived today, and what they mean
- how storytellers were important people in Anglo-Saxon England
- how some rich Anglo-Saxon women were powerful people.

Look in 'Digging Deeper, Living in Anglo-Saxon England'.

A Viking case study

Why did the Vikings travel from their homelands and where did they go?

The Vikings **raided** and settled in many lands. The people of these lands had different names for them. The English called them Danes or Northmen. Today, they are called Vikings.

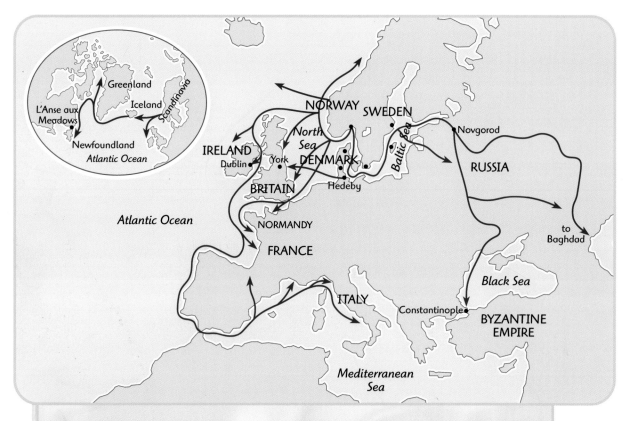

The Vikings came from Denmark, Norway, and Sweden. In search of trade, they travelled to many parts of Europe and beyond to the Near East.

Looking for a new start

The Vikings were always looking for new land to settle in and farm. Britain had good farmland, so the Vikings settled in Britain and set up their own kingdoms. By 870, the only English kingdom that did not belong to the Vikings was the kingdom of Wessex.

How did the Vikings travel so far?

The Vikings left their homelands in ships. The sight of their **dragonships** approaching frightened people all over Europe. These ships were longer and stronger than any other ships. They had at least 32 oarsmen and a large sail. As they came closer, people on land would see the frightening figures carved on the **prow**.

Viking dragonships could sail in bad storms and in shallow water, and were light enough to be lifted across land. We know quite a lot about these ships because sometimes important men were buried in their ships. **Archaeologists** have found some of these burials. We know less about their trading ships, which were shorter and wider.

Exploring further

Use the Heinemann Explore CD-ROM or website to find out more about:

- how Viking warships were built

- Viking trading ships, which were built differently from Viking warships.

Look in 'Digging Deeper, Ships of the Vikings'.

This carved wooden post in the shape of a dragon's head came from the front of a Viking **longship**.

When did the Vikings come to Britain to raid and to stay?

The Vikings first started **raiding** Britain in the late 8th century. It was only later, in the late 9th century, that they decided to make a full-scale invasion and settle here. We know where and when many raids took place because local monks wrote about them.

The invasion begins

In 865, a large Viking army **conquered** East Anglia, Northumbria, and Mercia. Hoards of coins buried at this time show how panic spread as the Viking army swept through eastern and northern England. This was far more than a raid. The Vikings had come to stay.

This is a Viking **warrior's** metal helmet. A warrior's helmet was very important to him.

An Old English poem, *The Battle of Maldon*, describes what happened when Viking raiders came face to face with the local people. This battle was in 991.

On the beach there stood, calling out harshly
A spokesman of the Northmen; he spoke these words ...
'This tough crew of seamen sent me to you.
They've instructed me to tell you to send at once
Arm-rings in return for safety ...
With your money we will return to our ships ...'
Byrhtnoth spoke, he raised his shield ...
Angry, determined, he spoke these words.
'Here stands a nobleman, fearless among his followers
Who intends to defend his native land ...'

The Vikings did not write much about themselves. A lot of what we know comes from the *Anglo-Saxon Chronicle*. This account was written by monks in about 891. It emphasizes the violence of the Vikings, because they had attacked their monasteries.

Wessex stands alone

By 870, all the kingdoms in England except Wessex were controlled by the Vikings. The King of Wessex, Alfred the Great, stopped the Vikings taking his land. The Vikings settled in the kingdoms they had won. This area was called the **Danelaw**.

Exploring further

Use the Heinemann Explore CD-ROM or website to find out more about:

- the Viking invasions. Look in 'Media Bank' for an animated map.

Why were monasteries good places to raid?

After they landed in England, the Vikings often headed for the **monasteries**. These places had many treasures and lots of food and drink.

Life in the monasteries

Monks were men who lived in monasteries who had decided to spend their lives **worshipping** God. They did not marry and gave up their possessions. The monks' days were very full. They were in church for about four hours a day. They had four more hours to read and pray, and six hours to work. They would work on the farm, in the workshop making precious objects to use in church, or they would write out copies of the Bible and prayer books.

Well-known monasteries

Some English monasteries were well known abroad. Many people in Europe knew about the monastery at Lindisfarne, an island off the coast of Northumbria. It was famous for its wealth.

This silver and gilt chalice was made in the 8th century, to be used in church services. It is decorated with gold. It shows how precious the treasures in monasteries were.

An easy target

Monasteries were easy to attack. The monks who lived there were holy men, not **warriors**. They did not know how to fight the invaders.

Good sources of wealth and food

Monasteries were full of books, relics, pictures, precious objects, and gold that the Vikings could steal. They also had stores of food, which they kept to give to the poor and to travellers.

Lindisfarne and Jarrow

In 793, Vikings **raided** the monastery at Lindisfarne. They burned its buildings, stole its treasures, and killed the defenceless monks. In 794, they raided the monastery at Jarrow. Again, they had come to steal, burn, and kill.

In the late 7th century, a fine monastery was built at Jarrow, in Northumbria. It was the first building to be built in stone since Roman times. The walls were painted and the windows had glass. The monk Bede lived and worked here.

What evidence is there that the Vikings settled in Britain?

We know about the Vikings in Britain from written sources, and from things that **archaeologists** have found.

Viking sagas

The main written sources are the ***Anglo-Saxon Chronicle***, written by English monks, and Viking **sagas**. Sagas were long stories about Viking history that were passed down through Viking families for many years. After 1200, some sagas were written down. The *Orkneyinga Saga* tells about the Viking invasion of the islands off the north of Scotland. It tells of people who lived in Viking times.

Jorvik

The biggest Viking site that archaeologists have found is in York. In Viking times the city was called Jorvik. It was the capital of the new Viking kingdom. The Vikings built new houses, farms, and workshops at Jorvik. By 1000 there were about 10,000 people living there.

Exploring further

Use the Heinemann Explore CD-ROM or website to find out more about:

- a Viking saga about a battle. Look in 'Written sources'.

- 'Viking pastimes. Look in 'Everyday Life, Written Sources'.

- Viking objects, such as carved pieces used for playing board games. Look in 'Digging Deeper'.

Word detective

Place names

Viking words can still be seen in some place names in England today. They tell us what the place was like. For example:

-beck = stream	-booth = hut
-by = village	-gil = narrow valley
-holm = island	-thorp = small village
-thwaite = clearing	-toft = farm

See for yourself

Jorvik

You can visit the Jorvik Viking Centre, in York to see how the Vikings lived and worked. The Vikings lived in small wooden houses. Posts held up the thatched roofs. There were no windows and little furniture. Straw was put on the earth floor.

Many skilled craftworkers lived in Jorvik, selling their goods from shops. Weavers worked with cloth. **Turners** made wooden bowls and cups. Metalworkers worked with gold, silver, and copper. Jorvik was an important centre of trade.

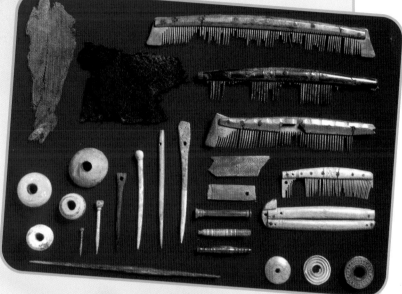

Many Viking objects have been found in York. In a place called Coppergate, bits of food have been dug up, as well as wooden and leather objects. Bones of animals, such as pigs, chickens, and deer, have been found, as well as fish bones, egg and nut shells. The wet soil stopped these things from rotting away.

An ordered society

Once they had settled in their new land, the Vikings showed that they could live peacefully. Under the king, there were three main groups. The top men called jarls, or earls, ruled over large areas of land for the king; there were only a few of them. Most Vikings were freemen, or karls. They were farmers, craftsmen, and warriors. Lastly, there were the slaves, or thralls. Who did all the hard jobs. They were criminals or prisoners from other countries.

Farming and trade

Most Vikings in Britain were farmers. They set up many new villages and farmed the land. They took some of their goods to Viking towns to trade for other things. Many Viking goods went to other countries. Traders sold wood, iron, and furs in exchange for things like gold, silk, and jewels.

Exploring further

Use the Heinemann Explore CD-ROM or website to find out more about:

- evidence of Viking games and sports
- Viking art and fashions.

Look in 'Digging Deeper, Living in Viking Britain'.

The Vikings lived in halls. These were copies of the halls of Anglo-Saxon lords. This description of life in a Viking hall comes from a Viking story called *Grettir's Saga*. It was written in 1320.

In those days farmsteads usually had large halls in them. The men sat by the fire in the evening. Tables were put up in front of them at mealtimes. After meals, they lay down and slept near the fire. During the day, women worked there weaving with wool.

This stone cross at Gosforth in Cumbria shows the mix of Viking pagan and Christian beliefs. The Christian crucifixion is carved on one side. On the other side are scenes from a story about pagan gods.

Beliefs

The first Vikings often mixed Christian and **pagan** beliefs. Many Viking objects have been found in English rivers. They were probably **sacrifices** made to pagan gods. By about 1000, many Vikings in northern England had become Christians. This was helped by their kings becoming Christians. The kings punished people who kept **worshipping** the pagan gods.

This pagan Viking grave comes from Orkney, in Scotland. The Vikings became Christians soon after they settled here.

Where did the Vikings finally settle in England?

By 870, the Vikings ruled all the kingdoms of England except for Wessex. The King of Wessex, Alfred the Great, was determined to stop their advance.

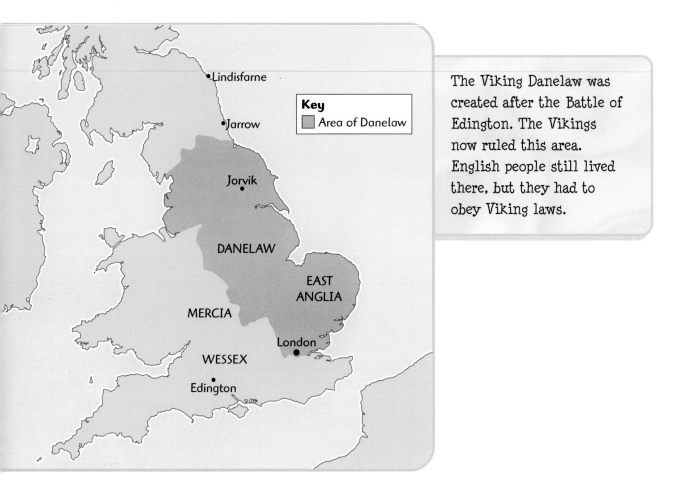

Key
■ Area of Danelaw

Lindisfarne
Jarrow
Jorvik
DANELAW
EAST ANGLIA
MERCIA
London
WESSEX
Edington

The Viking Danelaw was created after the Battle of Edington. The Vikings now ruled this area. English people still lived there, but they had to obey Viking laws.

Alfred the Great

Alfred became King of Wessex in 871. In 878 he led his forces in a great victory against the Vikings at Edington in Wiltshire. Alfred and the Viking leader, Guthrum, agreed to divide England between them. Alfred would rule the west, Guthrum would rule the **Danelaw**.

In the 890s new Viking raiders attacked Wessex. Alfred had improved his army and built many **fortified** towns, called **burhs**. He also built warships to fight the Vikings at sea. He defeated the Vikings and stopped them **conquering** the whole of England.

This jewel shows Alfred the Great. It was found in Somerset and probably belonged to him. The words round the outside say, 'Alfred had me made'.

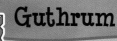

Guthrum

Guthrum was a great Viking leader. He arrived in England around 871. After his defeat by Alfred at Edington, Guthrum became a Christian and changed his name to Athelstan. He ruled East Anglia until his death in 890.

The creation of England

After Alfred died, his son Edward and daughter Aethelflaed won back land from the Vikings. By the end of Edward's reign in 924, he controlled most of the Danelaw. Welsh princes, the kings of the Scots, and the leaders of the Northumbrians also obeyed him. Edward 'the Elder' was overlord of all England.

A second invasion

In 980, a new wave of Viking invasions began. King Ethelred II of Wessex gave the Vikings £10,000 to stay away from England. This money was called **Danegeld**. However, the Vikings kept coming back. After Ethelred died in 1016, his son Edmund agreed with the Viking leader Cnut to split England between them. But Edmund died, and Cnut became King of all England. He remained King of England, Denmark and Norway until 1035.

Timeline

55 and 54 BC	Julius Caesar leads unsuccessful invasions of Britain
AD 43	Roman invasion of Britain begins
47	Maiden Castle **hill fort** is captured by the Romans
50	Roman city is founded at London
51	Caratacus is captured by the Romans
60	Boudicca leads her forces in **revolt**
c70s–160s	Lowland Britain becomes **romanized**
122	Hadrian's Wall is begun, to protect northern England from the Picts and Scots
313	Emperor Constantine allows Christians to worship freely in the Roman **Empire**
400–500	Picts, Scots, Saxons, Angles, and Jutes invade Britain
c407	Roman soldiers have been withdrawn from Britain by now; Roman rule ends
after 500	Anglo-Saxon kingdoms of Wessex and Kent become powerful
597	Augustine arrives from Rome to convert the people of Britain to Christianity
c624	An important **pagan** ship burial takes place at Sutton Hoo
635	A **monastery** is set up at Lindisfarne
c650	The Anglo-Saxon poem *Beowulf* is written
731	Bede completes his *History of the English Church and People*, at Jarrow monastery
793	Vikings attack Lindisfarne, beginning Viking conquests in Britain
871–899	Alfred the Great is King of Wessex
878	Alfred's forces defeat Viking forces led by Guthrum at the Battle of Edington
910–920	King Edward and Queen Aethelflaed re-**conquer** most of the lands held by the Vikings
919	Vikings found the city of Jorvik
980	A new wave of Viking invasions begins in England
1016–35	Cnut reigns as King of all England
1066	The Anglo-Saxon English are defeated by the Normans at the Battle of Hastings and the Normans take over England

See for yourself

Celts and Romans

Roman Baths Museum, Bath and North East Somerset
A **reconstruction** of the bath complex and parts of the temple can be seen at this impressive museum.

Burgh Castle, Norfolk
You can see the remains of the walls and bastions at this 3rd century shore fort.

Caerleon, Gwent
The best example of an **amphitheatre** in the country is here, together with remains of a legionary fort and a museum.

Chedworth, Gloucestershire
Much remains of this large Roman villa, including some magnificent **mosaics**.

Corinium Museum, Cirencester
This was the second largest Roman town, and the museum houses reconstructions, mosaics and many artefacts.

Fishbourne, West Sussex
There is much to see of this, the most magnificent Roman house in Britain, including mosaics.

Hadrian's Wall, Cumbria and Northumberland
The best preserved parts of the wall are between Housesteads Fort and Birdoswald Fort. The fort of Vindolanda, near Hexham, also has many finds in the museum.

Anglo-Saxons

Bede's World, Jarrow, Northumberland
Visit the monastery remains, an Anglo-Saxon farm, and an exhibition about the life of Bede.

British Museum, London
The treasures from the Sutton Hoo burial can be seen here.

Lindisfarne Priory, Holy Island
Visit the site of the famous Anglo-Saxon monastery **raided** by the Vikings in the 8th century.

Offa's Dyke
Much of the wall and ditch built by King Offa in the 8th century can still be walked.

Sutton Hoo, Suffolk
You can see the remains of the ship burial here, as well as replicas of the treasures.

West Stow, Suffolk
There is a modern reconstruction of an Anglo-Saxon village at West Stow, where you can find out what is was like to live in Anglo-Saxon times.

Vikings

Iona, Hebrides
There is a Viking burial ground here, as well as stone crosses.

Jorvik Centre, York
The centre recreates the sights, sounds, and smells of life in a 10th century Viking city.

Maldon, Essex
You can visit the site on the River Blackwater of the battle between the Anglo-Saxons and the Vikings, described in the famous Anglo-Saxon poem, *The Battle of Maldon*.

Museum of London, London
You can see a collection of Viking weapons and other objects here.

Museum of Scotland, Edinburgh
The museum has a collection of Viking artefacts from across Scotland, and a reconstruction of a grave from Orkney.

Glossary

amphitheatre an arena used for fighting and chariot racing

Anglo-Saxon Chronicle year-by-year history of England begun in 800s and continued until 1100s, written by monks

archaeologists people who dig up and study things from the past

artefact an object made by humans, especially one from the past which is historically important

bretwalda title given to a king who was said to have power over all of Britain

Britons people who were living in Britain before the Roman and Anglo-Saxon invasions

burh fortified town, first developed by Alfred of Wessex. It has given us the modern term 'borough', which is a part of a city with its own local government.

Celtic name given to people living in Britain before Roman times; the Celts started coming to Britain from Europe around 700 BC

citizen member of a country or empire

conquer to defeat someone

Danegeld money paid by English kings to Danish Vikings, to stop them attacking their lands

Danelaw land in eastern England settled by Danish Vikings, given them by King Alfred

dragonships Viking warships with a dragon's head carved on the front

dyke steep bank of earth built as a defence

emigrate to leave one country and move permanently to another

Empire (Roman) the large area of land ruled by the Romans. It covered much of Europe, North Africa and the Middle East.

export to sell goods to other countries

fortified something made strong to protect against attack

governor a Roman, usually a senator, in charge of a province of the empire

hill fort camp in a high place which was a Celtic town or iron age settlement

immigrant person who has come from one country to live in another

import to buy goods from other countries

Latin official language of the Roman Empire

longship Viking warship with oars and a sail

massacre to kill a large group of people

missionary person who travels to other countries to convert people to their religion

monastery place where monks live

mosaic floor pictures made from small pieces of stone

navigable able to be used by boats

nobles rich and important people

pagan used by Christians to describe people who worshipped non-Christian gods

primitive at an early stage of development

prosperous successful or rich

province territory within an empire

prow the front end of a ship

pyre pile of wood to be set on fire, for burning a body

raid to attack suddenly and steal from others

reconstruction something built to look the same as it would have done in the past

refugee person who is forced to flee their country

revenge harming someone because they have harmed you

revolt a rebellion against the rulers of a country

romanized following the Roman way of life

sacrifice offering to the gods

saga long story about Viking history, sometimes written down

torque necklace of twisted metal

tribe group of people, often related to each other, sharing a way of life and a leader

turner craftworker who make objects out of wood

villa farm with a house and outbuildings, or a big country house

warriors Anglo-Saxons who fought in battles for their lord or king. They were rewarded with gold or silver.

woad blue dye with which Celtic warriors painted their skin

worship praising and showing respect for God, or the gods. It may involve singing, praying and doing things in a special way

Index

Titles in the *New Explore History* series include:

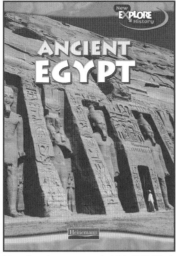

Hardback   0 431 07902 1

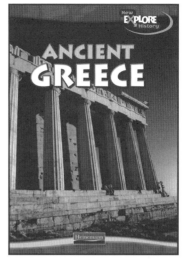

Hardback   0 431 07905 6

Hardback   0 431 07907 2

Hardback   0 431 07903 X

Hardback   0 431 07904 8

Hardback   0 431 07906 4

Find out about other titles from Heinemann Library on our website www.heinemann.co.uk/library